Suhriday

VAISHNAVI PATEL

BookLeaf
Publishing

Presentation by *BookLeaf Publishing*

Web: www.bookleafpub.com

E-mail: info@bookleafpub.com

ISBN: 9789357445788

First edition 2023

भावनात्मक पौधा

मेरी प्रतिकृति मुझे तीस साल पहले
इसी दिन मिली थी
मेरी फूल सम बेटी वैशु
हमारे चेहरे की रौनक वे
ज़िन्दगी की मिठास उसी थाली में
मेरे जीवन में अटक गयी
मेरी प्यारी बेटी की मुस्कान
खुद विधाता ने सौंपा हुआ
मेरा सबसे परिपक्व रिश्तेदार

Auction

My people were the only ones who conducted
the auction
Respect is what only strangers do.

Two sides

3

Be careful a little bit, human!
Not just coins,
A person also has two sides.

Poverty

Oh Oh, Poverty!
Is sacrificed in your troubles
While many humans may curse you.
You may catch the evil eye
Know when?
What will happen to you?

But No!
How do you know?
Because you are
Human eater!

When and where were you born?
Aren't you perishable?
Why I'm explaining to you!

O, Empress!
You are this- The one who kills the world.

A question

5

A soul asked,
Look at yourself and tell me the truth
Oh, human of earth,
If all the belonging you have to leave behind,
Then why you are too much running for that!

Eclipse

Why do we feel
eclipse shadow
in the presence of
sun-like sun ?!

Demand of nature

The art of being less miserable than we are and
the feeling of Being happier than being is
the Demand of nature.

How much more?

How much to explain to those who do not
understand!
leave it Let go,
how much to tell them now,
Would it make a difference
if it weren't for life,
Staying so different,
see how much you will live,
They had a habit of getting annoyed,
If it erupts by itself,
how much to convince it now,
It feels a little comfortable sitting like this on the
seaside,
How much we cry for the stone heart that
became,
There was nothing in love with nature today,
What a wonderful touch of air!
We were sold out at the price of emotion,
How much more wandering in the bargaining
now!

True Astrologers

9

There are only two true astrologers in this world.
A mother who understands the mind &
A father who recognises the future.

Middle Class

Half disguised as rich and Half disguised as poor
The class that celebrates the brotherhood of life
is- The middle class.

I don't want to be the daughter

Don't make me a daughter, Lord.
Don't make me a daughter.
My upcoming lives, don't make me a daughter.

Hanging between two houses,
Nowhere is my whole life written.
Don't do a daughter.

Raised my children like beautiful flowers.
Though they got their father's name.
Don't do a daughter.
Lord don't do me a daughter again.

Childhood

As a child, I was often asked
What I would become when I grew up?
Now the correct answer I got,
To be a child of childhood again.

That's why I Knock

I feel like I am who I'm, that's why I knock.
I walk straight so knock
No scam on balance sheets
I keep it clean, that's why I knock.
Yours sincerely, not to move on.
I'm having fun in my own world that's why I
Knock.
Keeping eye on me, ignoring me.
No, I don't steal. That's why I knock.
I won't take a bribe under the table.
If I come to you I will piss you off.
That's why I knock.

Mirror

Human only wants to see beauty in the mirror.
Not the truth!

The last visit of old age.

That's where to go next!
Let's go back
Let's colour this life with the colours of each
other!
How long will we continue to cultivate these
flowers,
Let's make those flowers bloom now!
Life is a match of happiness and sorrow,
Laugh a little and cry a little,
Let's play this game too!
Leave this stick of old age,
Let's get together and give deliverance to this
stick!
You and I have no idea how long this breath will
last,
But before we die, let's dig the grave of old
memories once again!

Emotion

There was a time of emotion!
When leaving the station
The eyes used to get wet and now
Even in the graveyard, the eyes are empty.

Poet

I have become a poet to embellish feeling
I have become a poet to decorate words.
I am constantly suffering from loneliness

That is why! I have become a poet to persuade
the mind.
Love, Joy, Grief, Emotion and Pain
I have become a poet to put everything down on
paper

Every day between the fall of the sacraments,
I become a poet to save the culture
I endured the wounds of love,
I have become a poet to hide tears.

Kindness

Knowing someone's compulsion
Making fun of someone's good dead
Don't call it kindness.

For an hour of helplessness
Showing two moments of happiness
Don't punish him for life.

He will get his deeds,
If there is sin, he will suffer;
Don't be a decision-maker.
Gem is always Gem (the precious)
To change the fate of the past
Don't name yourself a God!

Collection

19

Oh, God!
The wind of death has gone like this here today,
As if the merchant has come for collection
penny of breath.

Shape

Water has no shape or aroma,
Even air has no shape or form, colour or
fragrance.
"So what is sin or virtue?"
Or do you have faith?
Then there is betrayal, lying, theft or dishonesty?
No ...!
None of this has its shape or form, colour. It can
only be felt or touched."
Then why the earthen man-made by God
For?
For what work? Creates Discrimination !!!

I give you a chance to be human

Leaving any religion, I give you a chance to
become a human being.
Awake, human being.

The doctor - nurse tries to save your relative's
life without caring for his own life and you
question his service.
Wake up man.
I give you a chance to be human.

The situation of the people has been taken
advantage of even when they are rushing to save
their relatives.
Wake up man.
I give you a chance to be human.

If you are going to come to me empty-handed,
show humanity - be helpful.
Wake up man.
I give you a chance to be human.

On the one hand small children are sleeping
hungry and you are going to parties and
vacations.

Wake up man.
I give you a chance to be human.

Instead of cooperating with everyone in such a
difficult situation, they blame each other.
Wake up man.
I give you a chance to be human.

Instead of writing in the paper that everyone gets
courage, he writes what the government-
administration is doing.
Wake up man.
I give you a chance to be human.

The pain of losing someone is called paralysed
ask who has lost everything.
Wake up man.
I give you a chance to be human.

Wearing masks, staying away from each other is
often said to be stubborn.
Wake up man.
I give you a chance to be human.

This is the time where you give up your
stubbornness, resentment, anger, greed and give
yourself a chance to become a human being.

Listen man, I also give you a little hearing ...
wake up man ...
I give you a chance to be human